Camille Vérité

Jennifer Lagier

FUTURECYCLE PRESS

www.futurecycle.org

Published by FutureCycle Press
Lexington, Kentucky, USA

ISBN 978-1-938853-73-9

For the ghost of Anaïs Nin

Contents

Art of the Wild

Camille purrs and arches her back.
The artist, who is also her lover, paints a forest,
jungle-green circles around swollen breasts.
With one finger, he daubs orange over each nipple,
sensual bull's-eyes which harden, welcome his touch.

As she stretches catlike across his sofa,
he transforms her into a reclining zebra,
streaks her rib cage black and white.
Her thighs open like bright blue butterflies,
reveal the shocking pink secret inside.

Camille Behind the Wheel

She slips into a leather halter top,
pair of cutoffs, strappy stilettos.
Slides into her Jaguar convertible,
ready to travel, hit the road
for today's Big Sur adventure.
"Going to California" at high decibel
her choice of soundtrack.
Accelerates down Highway One
toward Nepenthe for blinis,
a juicy Ambrosia burger.
Tailgates poky tourists.
Flips off an obnoxious trucker.
Streaky hair tousled by wind,
her mascaraed cat eyes hidden
behind Versace glasses.
Hungry and on the prowl
for a bohemian afternoon
with a throw-away lover.

Camille and the Criminal Element

Bad boys seduce her.
Tattooed teenage criminals
expelled for boozing or doping.
The ones in detention who never
bothered with academics or sports.

These are the guys
who make her feel wicked,
inhabit hot dreams,
teach her how to sneak
out the window at night.

Sullen strays who take
what they want without
any sense of loyalty or obligation,
shun collars and leashes,
feed on what they take down.

Hoot and Holler

At the Running Iron, Camille struts her stuff,
demonstrates cowboy culture on the skids,
clogs, slides and twirls to a shit-kicker band.

It's Hoot and Holler night. Eagerly, she
encourages a barmaid with a pair of water pistols
to shoot lime juice, then tequila, into her mouth.

After more than a few, she's star of the bar,
ready to mosey down the street to Miss Lila's,
finally get that winking mermaid tattoo.

Exercise in Restraint

Camille sees him
stretched out on his back
against a thin rubber
exercise mat like
a luscious entrée.
His tee shirt
rides up, reveals
dark body hair against
pale, vulnerable belly,
a provocative trail that
travels south
to warmer regions
that tempt and intrigue.
As he performs slow,
sinuous crunches,
she is mesmerized
by what bulges
against baggy shorts.
Breathless, she imagines
straddling his hips,
riding him to
the finish line.
She is a sucker
for hardness.

Next Ex-Husband Interviews

Camille hands out maps and smiles
at the Concours d'Elegance
in Pebble Beach.
She has stationed herself
between two Rolls-Royces
near the Porsche Pavilion
where the richer boys roam.

Older trophy wives,
now gone to menopause,
glare as she flirts with their men.
Camille could have her pick
of international millionaires,
celebrity movie stars, local players.
As they examine each sleek, classic model,
she adjusts her tight tee shirt, licks her wet lips.

A Meal with Camille

She uncorks an icy
bottle of Mumm's.
Sets out the raw oysters.
Slips out of her panties.
Slides on a silk tunic.
Dabs a bit of perfume
on wrists and shoulders.
Lights the fireplace,
a stick of incense,
vanilla candles.
Starts Ravel on the stereo.
Puts beef bourguignon
on the back burner.
Lets the hollandaise cool.
Arranges asparagus
on her best platter.
Dips dessert strawberries
in melted chocolate.
Pulls back the bed covers.
Licks her lips.
Imagines the coming feast,
hunger sated
before night is over.

Peaches and Camille, Post Pinot Noir

Still tipsy from two glasses of wine and an Irish coffee,
she returns to the room, strips off her clothes, pulls on
a tight animal-print swimsuit, heads out the door.

When she wades, then slides, into the roiling hot tub,
children and their parents scatter. Out of the darkness
comes the red-bikinied woman she had met at the bar.

Side by side, the women allow their bare legs to drift
and flutter, soft shoulders coming closer, then touching.
They talk, share a bit more. One is blonde, the other brunette.

Later, as they meander up a single staircase, they giggle
at the resumption of unending rainfall, admire how
the alcohol has left them with no inhibitions at all.

Camille at the Creekside Café

The bill of fare is
what Camille considers
culinary foreplay.
Lets Ramon's recitation
of daily specials
tempt and arouse her.
Appetite piqued,
she savors his grin,
undivided attention.
Asks for something
satisfying and hot,
not necessarily a dish
on the regular menu.
Can tell he is eager to please,
will efficiently serve her.
Purrs at the salsa.
Praises his signature
breakfast burrito.
Eats every bite.
Knocks back a mimosa.
Is a generous tipper.

Camille's Half-full Glass

Within the bistro courtyard,
Camille contemplates her near-empty martini:
the first half turned to piss; what remains, bleary.
A thin slice of garnish floats in pale green vodka.

Soon she will swallow the juice in one motion,
a lemon slice joining others beside her glass.
The night is successful: live music, a tablemate
grinning, knowing, as she inhales the last of her drink,

warm and tipsy. His hand
is a perfect fit between her legs,
the blues guitar player riffing
as a sliver of moon rises through cypress.

I See Rumps

Camille performs
downward-facing dog
at the "Just for You"
yoga class,
tries to concentrate,
chokes back a laugh.
Around her,
lumpy men in sweats,
chunky women
in straining spandex,
asses high in the air.
She feels gravity
as it pulls
breasts and belly.
Knows she is
limber but vulnerable,
tush aimed
at the ceiling.
Feels a surging
hot flash as the
hunky instructor's
hands grip her hipbones.

Eternity Could Be Like This

Camille is barefoot.
Sits at her backyard
bistro table.
Sips an icy glass
of good sauvignon blanc.
Watches hummingbirds
as they whirr from
fuchsias to foxgloves,
promiscuously probe
deep inside open blossoms.
Imagines her lover,
supine with a
giant erection.
Fantasizes riding
him long and hard,
the scent and taste
of his pleasure.
She is content.

Teaser

Camille contemplates
the gardener:
tight ass,
intriguing jeans-bulge,
six pack abdomen,
muscular biceps.
Thinks of D. H. Lawrence,
his sensual women—
Connie Chatterley
with the gamekeeper,
a satisfying yet
unsuitable lover.
Rafael grins,
white teeth against
cappuccino tan.
She imagines him lightly
nibbling her nipples,
rough hands moving
against pale, silky skin.
Open thighs ache;
her back arches,
toes curl.
She quivers, feels him
push deep inside her.

Like a Leper in a Beauty Contest

Camille pumps iron
at the Wellness Center
three times a week.
Wears headphones
to extinguish
Fox News commentators,
Rush Limbaugh,
Bill O'Reilly,
red-faced and yelling
from all four TVs.
Cranks up "Dark Side of the Moon"
when the muscular
paramilitary guy
with racist tattoos
occupies a
nearby lifecycle.
He demands attention
as he rants,
recites lists
of who should
be exterminated,
deported or jailed.
Then invites her
out for a drink.
By the end
of her workout
she is exhausted,
worn out from
the effort of
biting her tongue.

Looking for Mr. Goodtime

After midnight in a Barbary Coast bar,
Camille sees herself reflected between tiers
of vodka bottles, whiskey, tequila.
A biker in black leather
bumps her stool, creating weird vibes.
His history is inked on brawny arms,
a still-oozing wound on the side of his head.
Camille's own roadmap is less visible,
but he intuits the general itinerary,
slides beside her, orders Jack Daniels neat.
Hey babe, he drawls, *you look like a girl
who could use some company.*
With one finger, he traces spider-web scars
crisscrossing the underside of her wrists.
They are castaways, seek the same alcoholic oasis,
another inevitable car-crash affair.
Now his hand caresses her thigh.
Go ahead, spin the chambers; tug the fucking trigger.
He pulls her closer, signals the bartender.
Honey, let me buy you a drink.

You Only Hear Them Sometimes in the Night

Camille hears them
raising hell
behind the bowling alley
in the parking lot
near her apartment
night after night.
Crack whores performing
noisy blow jobs
upon drunken johns.
Moans, beer cans
clanging into the dumpster.
Threats and yelling
during money disputes.
Alone within her bedroom,
unable to sleep,
she peeks out the window,
imagines an unavailable lover,
touches herself,
thinks of stray cats
in heat.

On the Town

The barista at Fermentations
shows Camille sixteen stitches
over her eyebrow, explains
how the local physician's assistant
sewed her up for only $35.
She promises an introduction,
Camille's insurance against
future tanked-up disasters,
says when she moves here
they'll be best buds forever.

At Mozzi's, old drunken hippies
play rotation pool.
Nailed to the ceiling,
a wagon wheel light, signs
from bankrupt local businesses.
Over-the-hill sluts shriek,
expose more side boob
than necessary,
take up all the bar stools.

A bright yellow poster
hangs on the door:
Guys: No Shirt, No Service
Gals: No Shirt, Free Drinks
Camille sighs, thinks
This is my kingdom;
these are my people.

Kryptonite

Camille contemplates her boy toy.
He sucks medical-grade marijuana
from a brand-new inhaler.
Later he nods off, snoring,
spills warm beer on her sofa.

This is not what she had in mind
when she took a young lover.
She notices overexposure
has diminished his luster.
Samson, now shorn, sleeps till noon,
anesthetized by vodka and oxycodone.

Superman has reverted to
a forgettable Clark Kent who
prefers unemployment, being in a coma.
Camille misses her man of steel,
the one capable of leaping tall buildings,
stopping locomotives, quenching her fire.

Roughing It

Camille sleeps on a red sofa
in a borrowed room she shares
with a John Lennon photo.
Tosses under skylights
admitting moonlight,
slivered glimpse of pine forest.
Red dust rises from the
dirt road just outside
her office window.
She is temporarily adrift,
earthly possessions in
three book bags, a duffel.
Alone, life is simple.
No interruptions, demands,
expectations of others.
Coffee brewed using a kettle,
single-cup drip cone.
Breakfast, the remnants
of a former guest's bagels.

Camille Vérité

She sits at the bar, scans her surroundings,
scents a few single men.
Ignoring the young and obvious,
she chooses a secretive lover, incognito,
checking him out from the shadows.

Every player understands the rules:
previous and existing claims are void.
She wants him, obsesses.
Tilting her head, she sweeps streaked hair
behind an ear, offers submission.

He approaches; she provides a gambit,
licks the martini glass rim.
Silently, he claims what he knows he owns,
presses his lips, hard, against her neck.
Teeth nibble soft flesh.

Put Out Water with Fire

Camille is pissed,
has promised
herself there would be
no more boyfriends, lovers,
especially not husbands.
Now she is hooked,
has it bad
for the newest
delinquent who
disrupts nights,
short-circuits writing,
hardens her nipples.
One more pseudo
Jack Kerouac,
Hank Chinaski,
or E. E. Cummings.
Hates her weakness.
Already knows
disappointment,
betrayal, major
heartbreak
are coming.

Camille Morphs to Crone

Watch her balloon
before your eyes.
Slender ribs disappear
under pasty flab.
Her sexy growl
sounds more like
a deep smoker's rasp.
Goddess breasts deflate,
unused, untouched,
nipples no longer perky.
Juicy nights discontinued,
fairy tales from the past.
Bikini wax unnecessary,
not worth the trouble.
Everything down there
in deep hibernation.
Time hasn't been kind.
She wakes late,
arthritic and cranky,
with leg stubble
and more wrinkles,
overpowered
by her own
morning breath.

So Long as It Comes Easy

Ah, the irony,
Camille reflects.
Her first week
of estrogen cream
and her partner
announces he's lost
any sex drive.
What's a girl to do?
she wonders.
Considers computer dating,
casual hookups.
Discovers the
Good Vibrations website.
Studies a column titled
"Kink for Beginners."
Researches toys to give
herself pleasure.
The Rabbit Pearl
(originally seen
on *Sex and the City*)
advertises pure bliss
for only $65.
She browses
for a new lover
among the
best sellers.

Casanova's

Lovers discreetly meet
in the Van Gogh room
which they have
all to themselves.
He orders mimosas;
Camille slides a bare foot
with scarlet toenails inside
the cuff of his Dockers,
caresses his calf.
The waiter nervously
refills water glasses,
refreshes sourdough bread.
Pheromones saturate the air.
His hands are invisible,
move under the table.
Camille is wide-eyed, speechless.
He is smoldering, seductive;
she, a mesmerized moth
addicted to candles.

Players

Within a week of online dating,
Camille has scored over 200 hits,
invitations for drinks, dinner, coffee,
a sunset picnic, walk on the beach.
Men compliment her smile, voluptuous body.
Share dreams of exotic travel,
romantic adventures in bed.
Promise indescribable pleasures.
Describe their sexual prowess
in excruciating, graphic detail.
Want her phone number, address,
employment history, love résumé.
Ask if she owns a car, apartment, or home.
Mention their current economic misfortunes.
At the restaurant, hand her the bill
while fondling her knee. Expect her to pay.

Acknowledgments

The author is grateful for the editorial assistance provided by Charles Rammelkamp and Gene McCormick.

Dead Snakes: "Eternity Could Be Like This," "Teaser,"
　　"Put Out Water with Fire"
SNReview: "Peaches and Camille, Post Pinot Noir"
The Potomac: "Looking for Mr. Goodtime"
Trajectory: "Kryptonite"
Wilderness House Literary Review: "Art of the Wild,"
　　"You Only Hear Them Sometime at Night," "Camille at the
　　Creekside Café," "Camille Behind the Wheel," "A Meal
　　with Camille," "Casanova's"
Word Riot: "Camille's Half-full Glass"

Cover artwork by Gene McCormick (genemccormickbooks.info); author selfie by Jennifer Lagier; cover and interior book design by Diane Kistner (dkistner@futurecycle.org); Calisto MT text with Bellota titling

About FutureCycle Press

FutureCycle Press is dedicated to publishing lasting English-language poetry books, chapbooks, and anthologies in both print-on-demand and ebook formats. Founded in 2007 by long-time independent editor/publishers and partners Diane Kistner and Robert S. King, the press incorporated as a nonprofit in 2012. A number of our editors are distinguished poets and writers in their own right, and we have been actively involved in the small press movement going back to the early seventies.

The FutureCycle Poetry Book Prize and honorarium is awarded annually for the best full-length volume of poetry we publish in a calendar year. Introduced in 2013, our Good Works projects are anthologies devoted to issues of universal significance, with all proceeds donated to a related worthy cause. Our Selected Poems series highlights contemporary poets with a substantial body of work to their credit; with this series we strive to resurrect work that has had limited distribution and is now out of print.

We are dedicated to giving all of the authors we publish the care their work deserves, making our catalog of titles the most diverse and distinguished it can be, and paying forward any earnings to fund more great books.

We've learned a few things about independent publishing over the years. We've also evolved a unique, resilient publishing model that allows us to focus mainly on vetting and preserving for posterity the most books of exceptional quality without becoming overwhelmed with bookkeeping and mailing, fundraising activities, or taxing editorial and production "bubbles." To find out more about what we are doing, come see us at www.futurecycle.org.